"In my Father's house are many rooms…
I am going there to prepare a place for you."
New International Version, John 14:2

"A wife of noble character who can find?…
She is clothed with strength and dignity;
she can laugh at the years to come."
New International Version, Proverbs 31:l, 25

A Funny Thing Happened on the Way to My Mansion

by Donna Holland

Illustrated by Lindsay Blumenfeld

Printed in the United States of America.
Published by Donna Holland, Jacksonville, Florida.
© Copyright 2016 by Donna Holland

Additional copies of this book may be purchased through most online book retailers and by request through major and independent bookstores.

ISBN 978-0-692-73486-5

Published by
Donna Holland
St. Augustine, FL
www.facebook.com/authordonnaholland

a funny thing happened on the way to my mansion

donna holland

Dedicated to my

beloved husband, John;

our daughters, Lisa and Mandy;

their spouses, Chris & Fred;

our grandchildren

Meredith, Emily, Lindsay,

Joshua, & Vivian;

and my dear friend Pam Amick,

who planted a seed.

INTRODUCTION

I used to think that I would be the next Irma Bombeck (a syndicated newspaper columnist whose humor was based on everyday life). In fact, I had often been told that I was funnier than Irma Bombeck. Well, maybe not often. But at least TWICE— once by my mom and once by a desperate daughter trying to flatter her way to Daytona for Spring Break.

Still, I thought I had all the credentials: English degree, a knack for hyperbole, and a wealth of knowledge and experience, ranging all the way from potty training to removing highly developed insect societies from teenagers' rooms.

But the years have flown by, and I am not the next Irma. I am still Donna Holland — wife, mom, Grammy, and writer of Christmas letters, in which I try to incorporate humor for the sake of the 25 out of a 100 people who actually read it.

A few years ago, one of my dearest friends said, "You should try to write a devotional with humor in it." I have been afraid of this undertaking, but I believe the Lord is calling me to do it, and I know he will equip me for His glory. No, I am not exactly the Proverbs 31 woman, but I hope, along with her, you and I can "laugh at the days to come."

Donna Holland

FOREWARD

The purpose of this book is to make you smile, so it is not a devotional in the true sense. I include Scriptures and prayers because I want to make it clear that true joy in this life can only come through a relationship with our heavenly Father through His Son Jesus Christ. Having said that, I believe laughter is a gift from God that brings relief, release and healing. As the writer of Proverbs asserts, "A cheerful heart is good medicine, but a crushed spirit dries up the bones." (NIV, Proverbs 17:22)

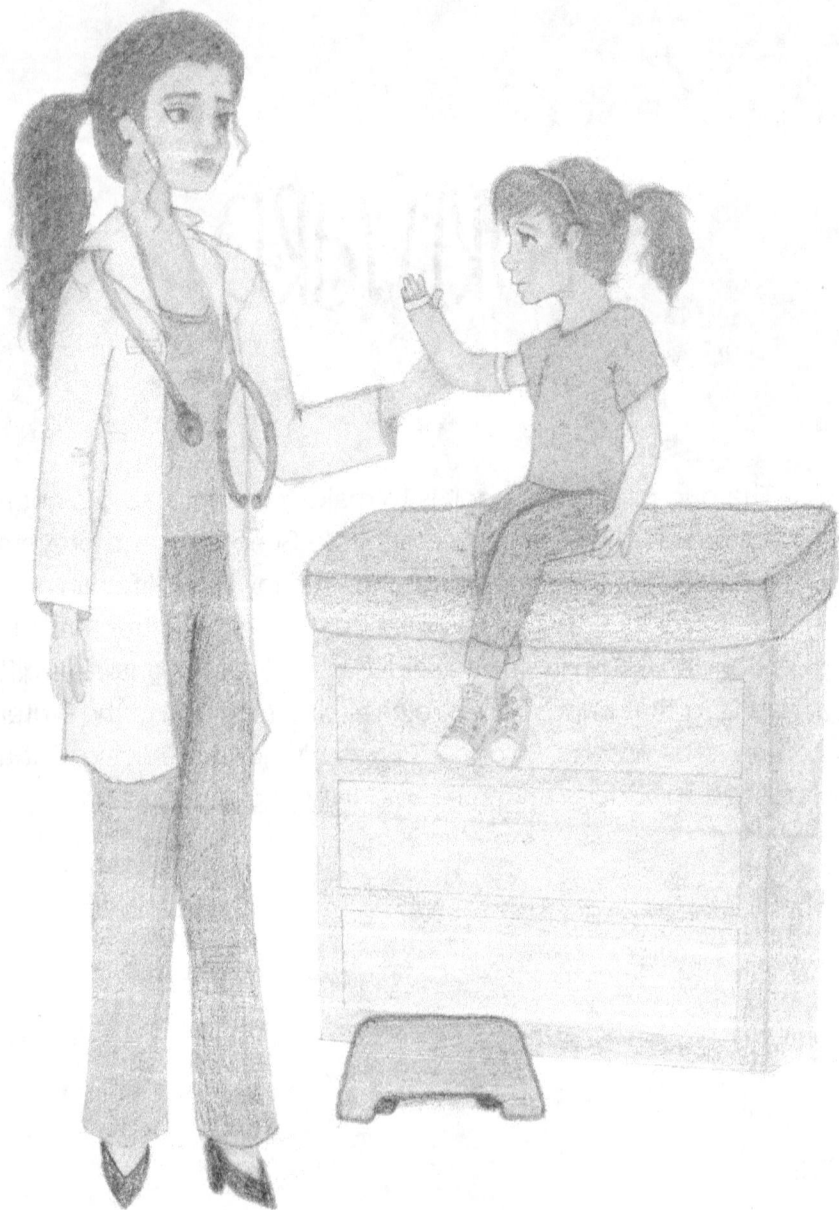

IS THIS REALLY
an EMERGENCY?

Here's the drill. You come home from the hospital with your precious newborn, and it's crisis time — the crying, the screaming, the wailing (mainly you and your hubby). Seriously, you don't know what's wrong with this little creature, and it's scary; so you call the pediatrician's office for an emergency visit. You insist that the doctor check your baby's eyes, ears, nose, throat, height, weight, temperature, heart rate, and head size. Your baby's fine, declares the busy, weary doc.

As time goes on, the emergency drills continue. You arrive at the doctor's office with your gravely ill, semi-conscious, barely responsive angel. At the very MOMENT you enter the waiting room, the horribly sick child who kept you up for 10 hours suddenly becomes the Energizer Bunny — running, jumping, laughing, singing, playing. Really? By the time you see the doctor, your child's symptoms have totally disappeared; and the busy, weary doc looks as if he wants to check YOUR head size.

Honestly, I have never been able to figure out this phenomenon. All I know is this: rush a near-comatose child to the pediatrician's waiting room, and he will instantly, miraculously recover.

"Let us then approach God's throne of grace
with confidence, so that we may receive mercy
and grace to help us in our time of need."
Hebrews 4:16

Father, thank You for the loving, patient physicians who care for our children throughout their childhood and who are able to calm our anxieties with their gifts of healing. Thank You that You are the Great Physician and that we can trust You with our children's health, welfare, and indeed, their very lives.

magic mommy

Okay, I never thought I'd be a "magic mommy" because I... well, I didn't like kids all that much. It wasn't so much that I didn't like children, but I'd had minus zero experience due to the fact that I was allergic to babysitting during my teenage years.

So, if children were supposed to be a blessing, why did I come home with my firstborn and immediately break out in hives, take to my bed, and cry for 24 hours? Can anyone relate to this? Seems motherhood would have to "grow" on me, which it did as I watched my husband feed, burp, bathe and change diapers. Thanks, Honey!

At any rate, the transition to parenthood can be quite a shock, especially if you're fond of eating, sleeping, and bathing on a regular basis. But I wouldn't trade those early learning years. I might not have been a "magic mommy," but I was quickly understanding the "magic" of my little Lisa. The Lord had blessed me with a precious (albeit HYPER) little girl, and He would give me the help I needed to deal with all this "magic."

"Train up a child in the
way he should go,
and when he is old he
will not turn from it."
Proverbs 22:6

Father, thank You for Your gracious promises to us through Jesus Christ and for all the grace You bestow on us as parents. Thank You for Your Word, which assures us of Your unfailing help in all our circumstances.

ABCs & Band-aid Knees

"Now I know my ABC'S"
Behold the toddler, if you please
Your gait starts out a bit unsteady
But wait you'll soon be more than ready
To run a mile, time to explore
Meanwhile we pant as we implore
"Slow down! Naptime is almost here"
But it's US who need the nap, we fear
Just can't keep up—you're everywhere
In drawers and closets, climbing stairs
You bang your head, you scrape your knees
Eat sand and dirt and leaves from trees
So many teeth for you to use
Alas, it seems they're just a ruse
Swallow it whole, you little elf!
You'd rather try to choke yourself
You whine, you scream, you sometimes bite
While we just pray you'll sleep all night

Time to put your toys away
Say good-bye to another day
Thumb in mouth and lamb in tow
Jesus loves you, this we know

I have to admit the model for this poem was my grandson, Joshua, who was 2 years old at the time of this writing and residing in Baltimore with his proud and EXHAUSTED parents.

The lamb was his bedtime "must have," and three identical lambs rotated from wash cycle to crib. Mom & Dad sang "Jesus Loves You" to him every night, and he could say, "Jesus," which also sounded just like "cheese." But who cared? Not us, and certainly not Jesus.

**"O Lord, our Lord, how majestic is your name
in all the earth! You have set your glory
above the heavens. From the lips of children
and infants you have ordained praise."
Proverbs 8:1-2**

Father, thank You for these precious little ones. May we always be faithful to teach them about praising their heavenly Father. Give us patience, wisdom and compassion as we guide them through these early years.

CELEBRATING TWINS

They came 12 weeks early and five minutes apart
And took all of five minutes to steal everyone's heart

All summer long in neo-natal I.C.U.
Respirators, monitors and feeding tubes

Sometimes they quit breathing & so did we all
Sometimes dropped their heart rates, and our hearts would fall

Twelve weeks later they were home, and we were all glad
They burped, slurped and cried (and that was just Mom & Dad!)

They frolicked, they colicked, they refluxed, they slobbered
Dad, don't ask for dinner — you just might get clobbered

No eating, no sleeping, no showers, no rest
Double work for their parents, but so double blessed

And now a year later so much they've achieved
Advancing to a point no one could have believed

Not only do they sit, roll, stand, crawl and babble
But a few days ago they were seen playing Scrabble!

As we gather today, we thank God for His grace
So perfectly mirrored in each girl's precious face

He nurtured, protected, preserved them from harm
They passed every test cradled in His right arm

So Happy One-Year-Old Birthday, Meredith & Emilyl
You have each made your mark so indelibly

We're so happy to be here to help celebrate
And watch with delight as you eat ice cream & cake!

"It is good to praise the Lord... to proclaim your love in the
morning and your faithfulness at night... for you make me glad
by your deeds... I sing for joy at the works of your hand."
Psalm 92:1-4

"For you created my inmost being; you knit me together
in my mother's womb... your eyes saw my unformed body.
All the days ordained for me were written in your
book before one of them came to be."
Psalm 139:13, 16

DOUBLE DIPPING

In 1998, we received a clever newsletter from dear friends announcing the birth of their first grandchild and declaring said child the winner of Best Grandchild Ever Born trophy. This made me mad. I thought, how am I ever going to top that? I did. Our first grandchild turned out to be TWINS!

The "preem angels" (Emily & Meredith) were almost three-months early and spent nearly that long in ICU where they finished "baking." They were born in June and by the end of August, they were home — lean, but fully cooked and able all on their own, with no supplemental oxygen, no constant monitoring, no doctors and nurses eternally hovering, to stay awake all night! Talk about proud.

Caring for twins in those early months really taught Captain and Mrs. Zombie, a lot — mainly, that eating and sleeping just really weren't all that crucial and that regular bathing was highly overrated. By the time the twins were 18 months old, Lisa and Chris had graduated from *Land of the Living Dead* to *Land of the Hopelessly Tired*... gosh, time really flies when you're semi-conscious. And after an exhausting year and a half, they were sometimes even able to sit down as a family and eat the same meal — applesauce and Cheerios! Naturally, my husband and I (Grammy & Papa) began to burn up the roads between our home and theirs because we wanted to be significantly involved in their lives — who else was going to help them incorporate new food groups into their diet, like ice cream and pizza?! Developmentally speaking, the twins had almost caught up to their chronological age... too bad I couldn't say the same for their parents and grandparents.

"Children's children are a crown to the aged."
Proverbs 17:6

"We will tell the next generation the praiseworthy deeds of the Lord, His power and the wonders He has done."
Psalms 78:4

Father, thank You for the precious gift of grandchildren. Help us as parents and grandparents to live godly lives before them. Bless them, protect them, and give them peace and joy in their lives through a relationship with You.

ON YOUR TOES
AND ON YOUR KNEES

Were you ready to be a parent? In the clear, blue, serene sky of your marriage, weren't you content? Were you prepared for that lightning bolt to strike and shape the forecast for the rest of your life: STORMY!

Look, I know it is serious business to mix metaphors, but I'm going to do it anyway — did we miss the Parenthood Entrance Exam? Was there a school that taught Frazzled Days 101 or Sleepless Nights Graduate Seminar? Because we missed it.

We did take a course with other prospective parents in which we practiced various skills on a doll that I'll call Little Jane. Little Jane bore absolutely no resemblance to a real, live baby; therefore, we were mercifully free to stick Little Jane with huge safety pins (pre-Pamper days). So, we sort of learned how to change a diaper; but that was about it.

The other vital educational components of dealing with children were acquired in OJT (on the job training). These essentials consisted of begging, screaming, pleading, praying, bribing, and the ever popular and our favorite strategy, "Because I said so!" Naturally, I'm being simplistic, because parenthood required more energy and prayers than we could have imagined......kept us our toes and on our knees!

"But as for you, continue in what you have learned and have become convinced of, because you know those from whom you learned it, and how from infancy you have known the Holy Scriptures, which are able to make you wise for salvation through faith in Christ Jesus."
2 Timothy 3:14-15

"Then our sons in their youth will be like well-nurtured plants, and our daughters will be like pillars carved to adorn a palace."
Psalm 144:12

Father, thank You for Your Word, which teaches us all we need to know about dealing with all the issues of our lives, including our dear children. Help us to be consistent, godly parents and grandparents.

Train 'em up

Remember the big, wide wonderful world of potty training? You beg, you plead, you threaten, you cry, you buy M & M's from Costco that will last two or three sessions. You try books, training pants, no pants, toys, potty reward stickers, Potty Time DVD's. Finally, you accept the fact that your angel will go to First Grade in diapers. But of course that doesn't happen. When the time is right, your child completes Phase Two in the cabana bathroom at the pool... high fives all around! The experts have told us that our children are fearful of letting go, afraid of losing a treasured part of themselves.

This reminds me of myself. As God trains me to "grow up" in Him, I wonder if I am also fearful of "letting go," of losing a part of myself I treasure.

"But whatever was to my profit I now consider loss
for the sake of Christ. What is more, I consider
everything a loss compared to the surpassing greatness
of knowing Christ Jesus my Lord."
Philippians 3:7-8

Father, thank You for the many opportunities You give us to help our children grow up. Help us to trust that You are training us to grow up into mature believers who treasure our relationship with You above all else.

WHO KNOCKED OVER MY TOWER?

Have you ever watched in horror as your children tried to bite, kick, scratch, scream and claw their way to the top of the sibling chain? Have you ever witnessed the unthinkable — your perfect ones devising evil schemes to hurt and maim each other?

Naturally, we hate to admit that peace eternal does not reign in our homes. We have read the books, attended the conferences, implemented the strategies. And what's the result? Heavy, wooden objects flying through the air and aimed at the nearest brother or sister! Ouch! We teach our children love, respect, forgiveness, reconciliation. But as our granddaughter Emily phrased it to her tormenting sister one day, "Merey, you are driving my nerves off!" Indeed. We pry them apart, explain compassion, send them to Time Out, and leave them to ponder the age-old question of childhood: WHERE, then, IS the center of the universe?

Of course, we all know that the intense sibling rivalry of childhood will one day give way to....the intense sibling rivalry of adulthood — LOL! Seriously, it seems there is an innate desire in each of us to be No. 1, no matter our age. May our children and grand-children see in us the desire to imitate Christ and His attitudes above all else.

"Each of you should look not only to your own interests,
but also to the interests of others. Your attitude should
be the same as that of Christ Jesus: Who being in very
nature God, did not consider equality with God something
to be grasped, but made himself nothing,
taking the very nature of a servant..."
Philippians 2:6-7

Father, thank You for the wonderful example of servanthood we see in Your precious Son, Jesus. Help us to live His attitude before our children and grandchildren, and help us as we strive to teach them to put You and others first in their lives.

IS THERE a ROOM MOTHER IN THE HOUSE?

Have you ever been a Room Mother? Your child is excited and of course, you are too as you gaze on the horizon of last-minute cupcake baking; long, hot, sweaty field trip taking; and solo party decorating. I mean, it's stressful. You call 45 moms and beg and plead for their help, only to discover 42 work and three have doctor appointments. Seriously?

Then, you recruit your husband for the Clown Toss Booth for the Fall Festival. The result is a fantastic plywood clown with a hole for V.I.P. faces. While soapy sponges are heaved at whoever's face appears at the hole (preferably the principal's and not yours), the children all run around on the wet, slippery cement floor.

Finally, guess whose child slips on the floor and needs emergency room treatment for a possible concussion?

This is all true, but I'm not complaining about this venerable calling. I got to spend more time with my children, and I really honed my cupcake skills. In fact, when my younger daughter went to pre-school, she inquired of the teacher who was giving out cupcakes for a child's birthday, "Are those cupcakes made from scratch?" Seriously.

And apparently, what goes around a few thousand field trips does come around. My older daughter is officially a chip-off-the-old-room-mother. Unfortunately, all the age-old problems of parent participation still exist. As I explained to her, you can lead another mom to the pumpkin patch field trip, but you can't make her drive.

"And whatever you do, whether in word or deed, do it all in the name of the Lord Jesus, giving thanks to God the Father through Him." Colossians 3:17

Father, thank You for all the opportunities to be involved in our children's lives. Help us to be imitators of Christ in all we say, do and think.

DON'T CROSS THAT LINE

Have you noticed it's much easier to set boundaries for your children when they are young? If you still have young kids, trust me on this because they will grow up to become teenage drivers. Look both ways before you cross the street; don't talk back to your parents; no TV until you have finished your homework – and of course, pick up your toys (except for Play Doh, which never truly gets picked up but sticks around [pun intended] for decades in the form of hard, colorful, microscopic balls all over your house). Simple guidelines (coupled with fear and threats of snack-deprivation) to nurture and protect our precious ones, right? (Sometimes they get a little mixed up, as when our 3-year-old granddaughter, Vivian, declared one day, "Mommy, Daddy's talking back to me!")

But everything changes when they grow up. The don't-talk-to-strangers admonition takes on new meaning when WE become the strangers! Seriously, though, when our children left for college, we set one boundary: a 3.0 GPA, or you don't take your car back to school. And we didn't budge. Our older daughter suffered the shock and dismay of her life when her first semester 2.9 GPA relegated her little Toyota to the family garage. As you can imagine, our standing firm made a profound impression on our younger daughter. Arriving home after her first semester in college, she tossed her car keys onto the counter and proclaimed, "Dad, I think I'll be needing a ride back to school."

"A wise son heeds his father's instruction,
but a mocker does not respond to rebukes"
Proverbs 13:1

Father, please help us to set proper boundaries for our children and grandchildren based upon Your Word, and give us the grace and strength to remain firm and consistent . Help us to be wise and discerning as we guide them to a deep reverence for You and to respect for others.

PICKING UP
OR DROPPING OFF?

Most of us have experienced the thrilling adventures of car-pooling at some point in our lives. Here's my definition of car-pooling: picking up (or dropping off) someone else's ill-behaved children, who then proceed to torment your amazing darlings on the way to/from school.

Yes, as your precious ones are polishing off the last bites of French Toast and trying to finish buttoning their shirts, the rude carpool kids have the audacity to ask why you are so late every morning. What nerve.

Of course, every carpool has what I call the Super Tormenter. In our case, Super T was Chad. Chad's contributions to our little caravan included, but were certainly not limited to, elbowing, pinching, yelling, littering, and just being really, really mean to the sweet angels who were trying to finish their homework in the car. Well, you get it. Sound at all familiar? What is a Mom supposed to do? Call Chad's Mom and inform her that her son is a menace to society? No... she might take it personally. (Even worse, she might refuse to drive on Thursday.)

At any rate, we somehow survived the slings and arrows of outrageous carpooling, with a lot of praying and tongue-biting along the way. In addition, I learned a valuable spiritual lesson: pray for patience, and you get... Chad.

"Whoever is patient has great understanding,
but one who is quick-tempered displays folly."
Proverbs 14:29

Father, thank You for the circumstances and people You place in our lives to teach us patience and to mold our character. Help us by Your grace to exhibit the fruits of Your Spirit in every aspect of our lives.

RULES FOR TEENAGE LIVING

When our daughters were 13, they were pretty typical teenagers, living by the rules of the age:

1) **It is forbidden** that a can of hairspray last more than five days;

2) **It is forbidden** that a 13-year-old girl wear a pair of hose more than once;

3) **It is forbidden** to make bad grades, but you must NEVER, EVER let your friends know you are actually trying to make good grades;

4) **It is forbidden** to make insects feel unwelcome in your room (accomplished by sneaking food into their rooms and faithfully leaving crumbs everywhere for their little guests).

I have about 413 stories I could include here that might convince you that people this age should be temporarily incarcerated. However, I simply cannot go into all the incidents where our teens demonstrated an intelligence so markedly (and suddenly) superior to that of adults.

I will not mention driving, dating, or curfews. And I certainly won't tell you about the incessant phone calls, the incessant hair dryers, or the incessant jelly beans clinging tenaciously to the $5,000 braces. No, everyone must discover these joys for themselves.

On a serious note, the teenage years can be trying times for parents and their children, but we need to lean on God's promises and His wisdom in raising our children to respect us and to honor the Lord.

"**Children, obey your parents in the Lord, for this is right...**
fathers, do not exasperate your children; instead, bring them
up in the training and instruction of the Lord."
Ephesians 6: 1 & 4

Heavenly Father, we beseech You for the patience and wisdom in training our children in every aspect of their lives. Help us to love and to encourage them in their faith and daily walk, and help us to remember that You love them even more than we do.

RULES FOR TEENAGE LIVING: 21ST CENTURY

Rule #1: Today's teenage girls seldom (if ever) wear hose anymore, especially to school. They wear tights, leggings, jeggings, tight leggings, skin-tight jeggings, and skinny jeans. If Mom's arm fits into the leg, the jeans aren't skinny enough (*Note: Supplemental oxygen is available in the guidance counselor's office.*)

Rule #2: Profile picture on Facebook must be changed at least twice a week, usually with a "selfie."

Rule #3: Unless they want to be locked up for terminal stupidity, they shall not text while driving. Otherwise, texting shall occur on a continual basis.

Rule #4: Hair must still be long, but half of it might be red.

Rule #5: They must spend at least three hours downloading music to their I-pods and at least 15 minutes doing homework.

Rule #6: Teens must not practice driving with a parent until his/her Drivers Education instructor has entered therapy.

Of course, some things never change. Overnight, comprehensive knowledge of the entire universe still begins at age 15 and now, thanks to Google and Yahoo, never ends. As grandparents of this techno-charged generation, we are blessed to be able to assure their parents that these teens will one day turn into human beings... and, yes, they might even turn into your best friends. Praise God!

"These commandments that I give you today are to be upon your hearts. Impress them on your children. Talk about them when you sit at home and when you walk along the road, when you lie down and when you get up."
Deuteronomy 6:6-7

Father, we praise You for the wonderful privilege of being parents and grandparents, and for allowing us to steer our precious children and grandchildren in Your direction. Give us wisdom and discernment as we speak to them about Your kingdom and kingdom principles.

This is MY room, mom!

Are you struggling to teach your children/grandchildren to keep their rooms clean and tidy? I can distinctly recall doing several versions of the cleanliness-is-next-to-godliness routine during my children's formative years, but as teens they clearly rejected sainthood.

In Lisa's room, Duran Duran and Rick Springfield stared out at me from every available wall, and clothes dangled from chairs, lamps, windows, mirrors — anything that didn't move . At least, I didn't have to worry about bugs in her room — nothing could have survived in that environment. And while I was concerned that the Health Department might condemn a small portion of our home, Lisa was actually PROUD of her abominable little niche.... so proud, in fact, that her room became a sacred dwelling place, where none but the elect could enter. I used to call myself Goldilocks because Teenage Bear always knew when I had violated the inner sanctum. "Who's been walking in MY room?" she would shout.

And of course, like all teenagers and their moms, my daughter Mandy and I were constantly at odds about her room. When she was about 15, I threatened to take away her phone (God provided this threat because it NEVER failed), and she really went to work.

Later, as I surveyed the wonder of made-up beds and neat shelves, I commented: "There now, doesn't that make you feel better?" She kind of chuckled (or was it snickering?) and replied, "No, Mother, but it makes YOU feel better." Ah, the wisdom of youth.

"The rod of correction imparts wisdom, but a child left to himself disgraces his mother."
Proverbs 29:15

"Even a child is known by his action, by whether his conduct is pure and right."
Proverbs 20:11

Lord, helps us to teach our children/grandchildren the right virtues, even in the mundane areas of personal pride and personal responsibility. Help us to pick our battles, and give us the right words and attitudes as we exhort them to do their best.

What's wrong with Blue lipstick?

Gosh, I remember a visit with my older daughter Lisa and family that sure brought back some memories. The twins were 12 and had swapped their dress-up magic wands for mascara wands. Lisa was chastising Meredith for overdoing her eyeshadow when I thought back to the time when Lisa was 12.

Having resolutely decided that I was the ENEMY, my daughter planted herself firmly on Daddy's lap, batted her eyelashes at NASCAR speed, and implored permission to use "just a little blush." I relented, bought the blush, and in a matter of a few weeks, she bore a slight resemblance to Chuckles the Clown.

In spite of my tearful reports to Dad, it is amazing how quickly he gave in on other items. Next came eyeshadow, in colors I knew hadn't even been invented. Then came the double-acting, all-purpose, 80-proof, wide angle mascara, which took a full hour to apply but only two minutes to smudge.

Next was lipstick, which Lisa claimed I gave her permission to use the day the anesthesia was wearing off from my surgery — didn't Mother remember? But it is so ironic how things change through the years. Now, I AM the one haunting the Beautypedia website for the latest in nuclear skin care. And I promise I am not making this up: the other day, I was strolling through Sephora and behold — a beauty advisor sporting the bluest of lipsticks, with eyeshadow to match... yikes!

"Your beauty should not come from outward adornment... it should be that of your inner self, the unfading beauty of a gentle and quiet spirit, which is of great worth in God's sight."
1 Peter 3:3-4

Heavenly Father, help us to remember that true beauty lies within and to impart this truth to our children and grandchildren. Give us wisdom and discernment as we set boundaries for their good and in light of Your will.

FROM KINDERGARTEN TO COLLEGE

Wake up, little one, it's almost time
Your school begins at 8:09
But Mommy, I'm just too tired to go
Wanna stay home and play LEGO
But your backpack's ready
And your lunch is prepared
Will you hold my hand, Mommy?
I'm really so scared

Hey, daughter, are you packed?
It's almost that time
Sure am, Mom & Dad
That campus is so fine
Well, you're all settled in
Your dorm room's your lair
Can you stay awhile longer?
Mom & Dad, I'm so scared

Gosh, don't you remember your children's first day in kindergarten? It's so exciting and so scary, for them and for us. You deliver your little, precious, perfect angel into the hands of a virtual stranger, and you cry all the way home. Then, in a matter of a few weeks, you're dropping off your grown and not-so-perfect-angel at college and cry all the way home.

"Find rest, O my soul, in God alone; my hope comes from
Him. He alone is my rock and my salvation;
He is my fortress, I will not be shaken."
Psalm 62: 5-6

Father, thank You for the blessings of children and for the wisdom You impart during their years of growing up. Thank You for the peace that comes from knowing we have brought them up to know, love and serve You.

abcs to sats

Did they just learn their ABC's?
And now it's time for SAT's
Where oh where their childhood thrills?
It's on to Math and Verbal Skills

Where indeed the Fashion Plates
The Legos, trucks, and roller skates?
Ready, set, accelerate
Now it's time to graduate

Yesterday was Play Doh time
Trikes and bikes and nursery rhymes
Soon they have to face the Test
Every college wants the best

Practice tests and online prep
Preparation marks each step
Must submit their highest score
Take it once and five times more!

Gosh, this moment comes way too soon, doesn't it? Yesterday, they were roaming their play-yards; tomorrow, they'll be roaming the campus. God bless and protect our children and grandchildren as they enter the precarious college years; they will need our prayers more than ever.

"He will cover you with His feathers,
and under His wings you will find refuge;
His faithfulness will be your shield and rampart."
Psalm 91:4

Father, thank You for your Word and its precious promises to those who hope in You. As our children and grandchildren enter the crucial university years, we trust You to protect and to guide them. Give them grace and strength to stand firm in their faith and to be a blessing to others.

aRE THEY REallY GROWING UP?

We all remember that glorious moment when we first beheld our precious, screaming newborn. We fondly recall the sleepless nights, the crying, the feeding, the praying.

How quickly they moved from infancy to teenager. And, yes, we again fondly recall the sleepless nights, the crying, the feeding, the praying. Seriously, we think they may never grow up.

But one day, it dawns on you that your child is actually showing signs of maturity. In the case of our children, this maturity began in college when they realized the family endowment was about to end and real life was about to begin.

These were some of the hallmarks we noticed:

1) Attending class on a semi-regular basis
2) Studying for an exam instead of watching "Rudolph the Red-Nosed Reindeer"
3) Asking for Fruit & Fibre instead of Captain Crunch

4) Mild curiosity about how to operate a stove
5) Morbid fear of rent.

Of course, they may become legal adults before they become functioning adults. You will see this transition occurring when they begin to understand that a job search takes longer than 20 minutes and that they actually have to fill out an application.

But they really do eventually grow up, and it is totally thrilling the day they grab the bill for lunch and say, "That's on me, Dad." If we suffer these growing pains with our children, imagine what grief we cause our heavenly Father with our stubborn willfulness and immaturity. But imagine His joy as He watches us grow into mature believers!

"Anyone who lives on milk, being still an infant, is not
acquainted with the teaching about righteousness.
But solid food is for the mature, who by constant use have
trained themselves to distinguish good from evil."
Hebrews 5:13-14

Father, thank You for Your everlasting patience with us Your children. Help us to "grow up" in our faith and to desire wisdom and sound judgment. May we look to You to equip us in our journey toward spiritual maturity.

mission possible

Heard a voice a while back from a very old tape
But it's still very clear and concerns my life's fate
So I'll play it for you and let you decide
Was I crazy or just a starry-eyed bride?

(Theme song from Mission Impossible T.V. show plays)

VOICE: *Good evening, Miss D. Our sources have infiltrated a rowdy group of young men operating on the campus of the University of Alabama. Their primary goal is to party and attend football games. One of their leaders, John Holland, appears to have potential but lacks stability and direction.*

Your mission, should you decide to accept it, is to marry this young man and follow him from city to city, state to state and country to country at ever increasing intervals until your address and phone number are completely disguised, even from yourself.

Should you or any of your children refuse to move, your friends will become totally bored and disavow any knowledge of you and your activities…. AND, you will have absolutely zero material for your Christmas letters.

Good luck, Donna. This tape will self-destruct when you purchase your last home.

Wow, little did I know that my "mission" would involve 12 moves. There was a time in our lives where we were actually "Wanted" in two different countries for excessive mail forwarding. Not only that, but our dental x-rays had been forwarded so many times that our dentist informed us that our teeth were no longer valid. Can any of you relate to this corporate way of life?

My husband would receive the challenge from his C.E.O., discuss it with me while I was asleep, then expect me to find a house and move in a week. Oh, okay, maybe it wasn't that bad.

However, during one of our last moves, I just knew that there was a very special nervous breakdown waiting for me, looking for me... but guess what? IT COULDN'T FIND ME! Neither could our friends, who swore we were in an address protection program. Seriously, though, I wouldn't trade my life's adventures, priceless memories and precious friends for anything. In every move, our gracious Lord has done "immeasurably more than we could ask or imagine."

"In his heart a man plans his course,
but the Lord determines his steps."
Proverbs 16:9

"Many are the plans in a man's heart, but it is the
Lord's purpose that prevails."
Proverbs. 19:21

*Heavenly Father, thank You for all the experiences and peo-
ple You have brought into our lives and for Your infinite care
throughout our moves. We acknowledge that our lives are in
Your hands and ask You to keep working in our hearts to achieve
Your purposes for us.*

IONG UNDERWEAR, HERE WE COME!

After 11 years of Florida sunshine
We headed to a slightly different clime
We exchanged our golf clubs & bathing suits
For ice skates and skis and those big furry boots
We moved to Ottawa — that's in Canada, you know
Where they play all that hockey and shovel all that snow
And while it was warm and snug in our bed
Outside the icicles danced off our head
While pals down in Dixie played tennis outside
Our driveway became a gigantic ice slide
And yet we got used to that cold, arctic place
Adjusted to numbness in fingers & face
With four layers of clothing and Polartec fleece
We discovered our frostbite would finally cease!

Gosh, what a change for our little Southern family. After 12 years of living in Jacksonville, Florida, my husband John accepted a promotion that moved us to Ottawa, Ontario in 1992.

Yes, this is the most traumatic move we ever made. Our older daughter Lisa was already in college, but Mandy was only 15. John had already moved to Ottawa, and Mandy and I were to follow in January. For some reason, Mandy wanted to spend her final days in Florida with her friends instead of packing and going to the dentist. And what about me? I mean, I was getting pretty weary of all the moving preparations, not to mention all the other responsibilities that John usually handled... I hated vacuuming and mopping.

But January finally came, and off we went to our new igloo. John's company told him we would be in Canada 3-5 years, or until we froze to death, whichever came first. We only lived there 3 years; but in fact, our DNA permanently froze in January 1994. Still, we loved our time in Ottawa, met many wonderful friends and learned that real men DO wear long underwear.

We had been told that we would not find a church like we were accustomed to in Ottawa, but God was so faithful to lead us to a wonderful fellowship at The Met. The friends we made there have been friends for life.

"If I settle on the far side of the sea, even there your hand will guide me, your right hand will hold me fast."
Psalm 139:9-10

Lord, thank You for showing us that you "will never leave us nor forsake" us, no matter where we live and no matter our circumstances. Thank You for Your infinite grace in times of need and trouble, and thank You for all those you place in our path to encourage us by their faith and friendship. Thank you for all those opportunities to minister to others, and continue to give us "willing hearts to sustain us."

OUT OF THE MOUTHS OF BABES

Memories of some of my children and grandchildren's most adorable words:

• When my older daughter Lisa was about 3 1/2, we were in church one Sunday when she began nudging me and whispering, "Mom, Mom…" I said, "Shhhh," but she kept nudging and asking, "Mom, what's a signo?" After repeating her query an exasperating number of times, I told her to be quiet and we'd discuss it after church. After the service, she asked again, "Mom, what's a signo?" I gave her a blank look, "What do you mean, 'signo'? She said, "You know, Jesus loves me, this *signo*."

• After many questions about heaven from my younger daughter Mandy and many explanations from me about how perfect things would be in heaven, her response was, "If everything is going to be so perfect, won't it be BORING?"

• When my twin granddaughters were 3 1/2, they were really pretty spiritual, asking many deep theological questions. One day Meredith inquired, "Grammy, how many teeth does God have?" Of course, I explained that God is a spirit but that Jesus had teeth like us. Later that same day, I asked Emily if she knew who the president of the United States was, and she looked at me with her earnest little face and replied, "God."

• On a trip to our home in Birmingham with my daughter Lisa, the 4-year-old twins and baby Lindsay, we stopped to change Lindsay's diaper. Meredith removed her seat belt, and Lisa told her to put it back on. My husband (thinking she needed a little break), told her she could leave it off.. Lisa told her she needed to do what she said, to which Meredith replied, "Well, you have to obey your grandparents. It says so in the Bible!"

• My granddaughter Lindsay was almost 4 when she asked her mom, "If Jesus is in your heart, how does He get there? Walk?" A little short on theology, but long on adorableness.

When my grandson Joshua was 2, he started belting out the Dolly Parton song, *Jolene*. (This was one of his mom's favorites that she sang accompanied by her guitar.) After a few lyrics, he declared, "Amen." Mandy smiled and explained that this was not a song that we usually end with "Amen." Hey, nothing wrong with a little religious fervor!

• A little story that my daughter Lisa related to me when the twins were 4: they were playing together one day and building a pretend house. Emily stated, "Looks good." Meredith responded, "Looks real, real good... we're building our house on the Lord Jesus Christ." Amen, little girls!

"Let the little children come to me....
for the kingdom of God belongs to such as these."
Matthew 19:14

Father, help us to have the child-like faith that You desire in your children.

a Jock In
mom's Clothing

When I was in my thirties, I picked up a strange notion. I began to suspect that there was another person lurking beneath the guise of wife, nurse, mother, tutor, chauffeur. Believe me, I treasured all those roles, but I sensed that somebody within was just itching to get out.

As I emerged from the mire of dishes and carpools, I decided to unleash on the world my great, though unproven, athletic skills (WHY was I always picked last in grammar school for the volleyball team?) Sure, I'd tried jogging, but that was not my idea of fun. I had faithfully pounded the pavements for several years at ever-decreasing rates of speed, and where had it gotten me? Every time I left the house, I lived in mortal fear of being recognized. Anyway, if I were going to sweat, at least I was going to enjoy it.

Spurred on by my husband's encouragement, I bought a new pair of tennis shoes, dusted off an old, decaying racket and presented myself to a local tennis pro. This was going to be a cinch. After all, tennis was just like ping pong, right? Thirty minutes later, I limped toward home—hot, tired, humiliated and with a gigantic swollen toe and blisters from the wrong size tennis shoes. As for my great athletic potential, the pro had gently explained that most tennis players take about five years to develop their games. Needless to say, I was no exception. As it turned out, it took me about TWENTY years! I was never as good as I wanted to be, but at least the pros stopped laughing.

I learned a great deal about myself in those years but mostly that my self-esteem did not depend on my performance (thank goodness!!). However, I have passed on my competitiveness to my daughters and granddaughters, and now we all enjoy playing together. We will do almost anything to win, but crying remains my personal favorite.

"Command those who are rich in this present world not to be arrogant nor to put their hope in wealth, which is so uncertain, but to put their hope in God, who richly provides us with everything for our enjoyment."
1 Timothy 6:17

Father, thank You for all those activities You give us for our enjoyment, but help us to keep an eternal perspective. Thank You that our self-esteem resides in knowing we are Your children and not in anything we can accomplish on our own.

Take a hike

I decided some time ago that I should trade my golf clubs in for a real good hiking stick. It's a lot cheaper, I don't cry as much, and nobody tells me to keep my head still. Happy trails, right? Well, sort of. But there have been a few mishaps.

One hike, I fell and banged up my knee, sprained my ankle, and tripped and spilled half the wild blueberries my poor, dear, precious grandchildren had risked their lives to collect. But with the help of the Lord and Celebrex, I proved that "you're only as old as you... are."

On another hike one June, the "Keenanites" (seven of our family in identical Keen shoes of different colors) experienced a terrifying thunderstorm. After being trapped under overhanging rocks for 50 minutes, my then 10-year-old granddaughter quipped when she saw a multi-legged creature, "You know, Gram, I used to be afraid of spiders, but after that near-death experience, they don't bother me that much." We can look back now and laugh, but when lightning felled a tree very close to me and my daughter, we were in serious prayer.

"Then they cried out to the Lord in their trouble, and
He brought them out of their distress. He stilled the storm to
a whisper . . . they were glad when it grew calm,
and He guided them to their desired haven"
Psalm 107:28-30

Heavenly Father, we praise You that You control all of Your creation. Thank You for being both our shelter and our deliverance in the storms of life.

I'M NOT TEEING OFF!

Have you ever wondered if it's a sin to play golf on Sunday? Well, guess it depends on how well you play. When asked this question by one of his congregants, the pastor gently replied, "My dear, I've seen you play golf. It's a sin ANY day!" *LA Times* writer and frustrated golfer Jim Murray was optimistic about the afterlife: "I'm betting that when St.Peter discovers I was a golfer, he'll step aside and say, "Go right in. You've suffered enough." I couldn't say it any better.

Like all my athletic endeavors, I took this up late in life when I was in my early fifties. I soon progressed from truly awful to slightly pitiful, although I did manage to break 100 a few times. As I've said before, I'm very competitive; so I spent many hours on the practice range and with the pro.

Unfortunately, I still experienced that annual rite of spring whereby I stepped up to address the ball and realized with familiar horror that my great golf game that never existed had totally disappeared. My husband had been playing at golf for many years but didn't get to play as often because, as ridiculous

as this sounds, he had a job. Still, we have worked since his retirement on taking our games to the next level, and guess what
we've decided? THERE IS NO NEXT LEVEL.

Now my vision is so bad that one day when we were playing golf, I waved enthusiastically to the people watching us from their condo patio. John just shook his head sadly. "Donna, those are flower pots." Oh, no wonder they didn't wave back. Still, this is an activity we "enjoy" as we experience together the beauty of God's creation along with some truly suspect golf swings. I won't pretend that I have never asked for divine assistance as I stared in fascinated horror at all the places my balls land. But Rev. Billy Graham, a former avid golfer, has stated, "...actually, the Lord answers my prayers everywhere except on the golf course." AMEN!

"Praise the Lord... Praise him, sun and moon,
praise him all you shining stars.
Praise him, you highest heavens and you waters
above the skies. Let them praise the name of the Lord,
for he commanded and they were created."
Psalms 148:3-5

*Thank You, Father, for the beauty and majesty of Your
creation and for allowing us the time and means to enjoy it.
We praise You that* ..."since the creation of the world God's
invisible qualities...have been clearly seen, being understood
from what has been made."
Romans 1:20

PRINCESS TALES

No time for snails and puppy dog tails
Let's hear it for sugar and spice
For ribbons and bows and ballerina toes
For everything pretty and nice

No time for frogs and dirt under logs
Let's hear it for ruffles and lace
For butterfly kisses and little Miss Prisses
With lipstick all over each face

For dolls and play kitchens and little pink mittens
Let's hear it for dress-up and shows
With little girls dancing and singing and prancing
Such talent as everyone knows

For easy-baking and fashion plate making
Let's hear it for French braids and curls
For Barbies and crayons and cottons and rayons
For rhinestones, tiaras and pearls

For contacts and braces and neon shoelaces
Let's hear it for lip gloss and rings
For bracelets of gold as they try to act old
With new hairdos and makeup and things

For feminine wiles, sparkling eyes, charming smiles
Let's hear it for laughter and tears
For as God has allowed to the humbled and proud
The gift of these girls through the years

No, we didn't have Little League or Pop Warner. We had dress-up, teacups, mix-ups, flare ups and makeup. But God knows our needs better than we do.

**"Every good and perfect gift is from above,
coming down from the Father."
James 1:17**

Heavenly Father, thank You for the gifts of our dear children and grandchildren and for the uniqueness of girls. Help us to model godly behavior before them as we teach them Your Words and Your Ways.

upload, Download, overload

Feeling perplexed?
You can e-mail or text
Conversing, you see,
Is so "last century"
Need info or help?
You can Google or Yelp
You can tag it, link it
Scan it or sync it
Need a form for your tax?
You can get it by Fax
Ever feel weary?
Just tell it to SIRI
i -Photo or Skype
You know the hype
On Facebook or Twitter?
You're a techno-critter

Honestly, did you ever think your life would be so consumed by devising, memorizing and hiding (especially from yourself) at least 542 passwords??!! No kidding, we have reset all our passwords so many times that we have had to resort to Chinese symbols! Look, technology is fantastic, and I'm not demeaning it. I mean, we have all the latest gizmos, too. And thanks to our granddaughters, we have learned the shortcuts to texting Nirvana. But admit it. Don't you long for an actual PERSON to answer your phone calls? I wonder if we "techno-critters" spend too much time on our smart phones, i-Pads, etc. and not nearly enough time working on our relationships with God and others. Just sayin'.

"Who richly provides us with everything for our enjoyment."
1 Timothy 6:17

"Love the Lord your God with all your heart and all your soul
and all your strength and with all your mind;
and love your neighbor as yourself."
Luke 10:27

Father, thank You for all the many ways that technology has improved our lives, for we know that every good thing comes from You. Give us the desire to spend more time with You in prayer and in Your Word; and give us a heart for others, especially those who don't know You.

SPORTS NUT

You might think you'd be reading about my husband, but you would be wrong. First, let me explain that the hand-eye coordination that my Dad successfully passed to my siblings was totally rejected by my DNA. However, the Spectator gene was, is, and shall always be a huge part of my makeup. I grew up watching all manner of athletic events on T.V. because both my parents were tuned in practically 24/7.

I recently celebrated what I considered a perfect birthday: watch the Senior Bowl football game at 3 (alternately checking on the golf tournament); watched basketball game at 7 (alternately checking on Winter X Games); watched Australian Open Tennis Final at 9:30 (alternately checking to see if I was still awake). When my daughter called and I told her I was watching the Winter X Games, she said, "If you weren't my mother, I wouldn't believe you."

My husband used to come home from his Monday night Elder meetings at church to find me immersed in Monday Night Football. What a lucky man.

"For physical training is of some value, but godliness
has value for all things, holding promise for both
the present life and the life to come."
1 Timothy 4:8

Father, thank You that we can appreciate the self-discipline and competitive achievements of many fine athletes. Help us to remember that spiritual training is more important than physical training and that the victory we shall win will be an eternal one through Christ Jesus our Lord.

COOKING 101

In our family, we have what is known as the "Cooking Hot Line." Usually, this means a desperate call from one of my daughters needing a recipe, technique, etc. Actually, now that I'm a mature woman, this sometimes means that I am calling THEM.

At any rate, when my younger daughter had been married about 3 years, she called the "Cooking Hot Line" to determine how to cook a turkey. Remember how insecure you were when you cooked your first (or thirty-first) bird? My husband's sage advice for cooking and testing for doneness: "Just tell her to throw the thing in the oven.... brown the breast; jiggle the leg; slit the thigh; and if the thing doesn't bleed, it's done." Thanks, Chef Dad. (Sure, you could use a meat thermometer, but why ruin the fun of all that suspense?!)

In yet another bid to be the family cooking expert, my hubby recently asked me, "Do you always put tomato paste in your Shrimp Creole?" "Yes," I said, "why?" Hubby: "I'm not a big fan of tomato paste." Me: "Oh, so you're not a fan." Hubby: "No, it's too acidic." Oh, okay.... so I guess he was PRETENDING to like my

Shrimp Creole all these years, not to mention chili, lasagna, etc., etc., etc. You get the point. I got even with him recently, however. He asked me on the way home from church what we were having for lunch. I told him I had taken something out of the freezer. He asked, "What is it?" I responded, "I don't know, but whatever it is, we're having it."

"May the Lord make your love increase
and overflow for each other."
1 Thessalonians 3:12

Father, thank You for giving us our life mates to love, support and encourage us as we walk together in our journey; and yes, thank You for the fun and humor we have shared through the years.

low fat & organic

I don't know about you, but I didn't start out cooking low fat, low carb, or low ANYTHING. Nope, I started out with DEEP — deep dredged and deep fried. But that was a long time ago, before we realized that all those yummy-smelling, yummy-tasting morsels were clogging our arteries.

Now I have progressed to grilled and broiled and, thanks to my daughters, to organic paradise. That's right. I now read every label, searching for those vile offenders that will compromise my grandchildren's health. Still, we as grandparents have a solemn duty to introduce our grandchildren to other options, such as doughnuts, root beer, pizza, ice cream, cheese crackers, etc. Otherwise, they will never realize what they are missing when we're not there!

Of course, I really do wish I had cooked more healthy foods when my girls were growing up. Yet, as I traverse the All Natural/Low Fat/Organic/Hormone-Free world of today, there is a nagging question in the back of my brain, especially in my olfactory nerve: can man really live without fried chicken?

"The Lord will guide you always; he will satisfy your
needs...and will strengthen your frame.
You will be like a well-watered garden."
Isaiah 58:11

*Father, thank You so much for guiding us into healthy
living and for providing us with the foods we need. Give us the
desire to crave spiritual food above all else.*

Camp Neveragain

My children and grandchildren love to camp, but I have no idea why, because I am deeply allergic.

When our kids were growing up, our one and only camping adventure began with a deep, vast, thick mud puddle that contained an apparent magnet for children. For some reason, muddy children, community showers, mosquitoes, and four people sleeping in a van just didn't cut it for me.

My idea of camping is lying on a comfortable bed and gazing out the window at mountains, trees, sky and other natural wonders; plus, I don't have to worry about bears. On the other hand, my husband at his tender age has recently decided the following things are enjoyable: bugs, snakes, torrential rains, mud, dried food, smelly campers and various other things that comprise the rollicking great fun of sleeping in a tiny, tiny tent on the hard, hard ground.

He and a pal have even hiked part of the Appalachian Trail. Obviously, hunger and dirt and freezing to death are on the Y Chromosome.

"When I consider your heavens, the work of your fingers,
the moon and the stars, which you have set in place,
what is man that you are mindful of him.
Psalm 8:3-4

Heavenly Father, we praise You for Your beautiful creation and the opportunities to enjoy what Your hands have made. Help us to reflect on Your eternal power and divine nature as seen in the great outdoors.

can you say, "paddle"?

Have you ever been rafting? It's really not all that scary — unless no guide is available, you have to help paddle, and you can't swim. Otherwise, you can usually overcome your sheer terror by focusing on all the outdoor hilarity engendered by your close proximity to huge rocks.

Of course, I'm exaggerating a little bit. My first rafting trip was on the Tukesegee River in North Carolina, with mostly Class 1 & 2 rapids, but with Class 100 kids and grandkids. Yes, we got stuck on the rocks a few times due to the ridiculously inept paddling of one of the crew.

Still, this first trip was pretty uneventful, and we all had the T-shirts telling us how much fun we had. Unfortunately, on another rafting trip, I shocked my kids and grands when I fell out of the raft; and with my usual poise could be heard for miles on the Tukesegee screaming, "Help! Help!" How embarrassing. I was rescued by a man in a kayak, while my not very amused husband glared and my frightened granddaughter vowed she would never go rafting again. *Note*: that same

granddaughter did go rafting again when they were staying at our house while we were out of town. Coincidence? LOL!

"He makes springs pour water into the ravines;
it flows between the mountains."
Psalm 104:10

Father, thank You for the rivers of Your majestic creation that provide water and enjoyment for your creatures and for us. Most of all, thank You for the Holy Spirit, the "living water" that flows from within all who believe in Jesus.

WINTER SPORTS

When we moved to Canada in the early 90s, we had record cold weather and record snowfall. Our hair froze; our eyebrows froze; body parts we didn't even know we had froze. What were we Southerners to do, ya'll? Winter sports, of course.

First, there was curling, which resembles bowling, except it's done on ice and is three times more ridiculous. You may have seen this on the Winter Olympics. More accurately, you probably turned it OFF.

Then, there was skating on the Rideau Canal, the world's longest outdoor ice skating area. We went; we skated; we conquered. Unfortunately, we didn't know how to stop, so we just skated until we fell down. Yep, hot chocolate tastes great with bruised ribs.

But the best of all our winter sports was downhill skiing. How does one describe the fun of donning huge, hard, heavy, tight boots, along with long underwear, socks, pants, turtle-necks, gaiters, sweaters, jackets, hats, gloves, goggles and skis? We needed a nap before we could even move, much less ski. Altogether, our skiing adventures have netted us a torn ACL, fractured fibula, fractured vertebra, broken thumb and near collar bone fracture. Do we still ski? Of course! We may not be dumb, but we are stupid.

> "God's voice thunders in marvelous ways;
> He does great things beyond our understanding.
> He says to the snow, 'Fall on the earth...'"
> Job 37:5-6

> "He spreads the snow like wool
> and scatters the frost like ashes."
> Psalm 147:16

Father, we praise You for Your marvelous creation. Thank You for the beauty and serenity of the falling snow and for the peace of Winter.

CHEERS, GROANS AND BROKEN BONES

When you have daughters, their athletic endeavors don't usually revolve around football or baseball. In our case, we had gymnastics, tennis, swim team and rugby. Nothing wrong with those.

Our daughter's gymnastics resulted in four trophies, two broken arms, and one dislocated elbow. Ouch....so much for the Olympics.

Then, there was tennis. Both our girls played as youngsters and still do. I was so excited when our daughter came home and said she was on the tennis team. She gave me a disdainful look and replied, "Mom, this is Canada; and I'm from Florida — of course I'm on the tennis team." Oh.

And of course, we have all the priceless memories of swim team. First, the thunder, lightning and storms roll in at exactly the same time for every meet. So, instead of starting at 4:00, they all start at 5:00. Your child then swims an event that lasts 2 minutes. You clap, you cheer, you wait 45 minutes until she swims again. After 85 events more or less, you are free to leave for a 10:00 dinner. My husband once remarked, "If I found out I had only one day to live, I'd choose a swim meet day 'cause the day lasts forever."

Then there was rugby... scary. The girls kick, push, punch, pound, tackle, knock each other unconscious. It was just plain thrilling to watch your kid having that much fun.

We somehow made it through the bumps, bruises and broken bones of their childhood, and more importantly, they did, too. Now they're parents themselves and can look forward to their own 10:00 dinners.

> "I will lie down and sleep in peace, for You alone,
> O Lord, make me dwell in safety."
> Psalm 4:8

Father, thank You for answering our prayers for the care and safety of our children as they strive to meet their goals in all areas of their lives.

TRAVELING WITH THE KIDS (OID VERSION)

I guess everyone has his/her recipe for successful (and peaceful) travel with children. When our kids were growing up, there were certain essentials. Food and beverages, for example, were a MUST.

As soon as we pulled out of the driveway, they would suddenly become ravenous. It didn't matter that just 10 minutes ago, they were feasting on French Toast and bacon. No, it was snack time, Mom & Dad. Snickers, Doritos and sodas were calling their name. I'd like to tell you we always brought fresh fruit and juices, but I'm trying to be serious here.

Another must included toys, games and books. Sometimes we played that ridiculous word game G.H.O.S.T., but my husband and I despised that game because the children always won (not that we're competitive or anything). Of course, the children never read the books we brought along, but they made great weapons for Mom & Dad. Naturally, we always had a first-aid kit because you know what happens when kids are constrained in a car longer than 10 minutes. You get scrapes, cuts, bruises, scratches — and that was just us!

Another necessity was packing TONS of clothes when we traveled. After all, we needed to anticipate climate changes and natural disasters, not to mention mind changes and un-natural disasters.

Finally, we always traveled with hundreds of maps because children get really grouchy when an 8-hour trip takes three days. "Are we almost there, Dad?" Seriously? Couldn't they think up a new line?

"The Lord will keep you from all harm — he will watch over your life; the Lord will watch over your coming and going both now and forevermore."
Psalm 121:7-8

Father, thank You so very humbly for all the many great times we have shared with our children and for keeping us safe in all our travels through the years.

TRAVELING WITH THE KIDS (NEW VERSION)

The goal is the same in the modern version of car travel, but the means are a little different. Food is still essential, but since one of our daughters is Mother Earth and the other is Queen Organica, they actually DO bring healthy snacks.

Toys, games and books are still a must, but electronics have replaced all that ridiculous real stuff. Remember the good old days of "Dad, she's on MY side!"? Now, it's "Dad, she won't give me a turn on the I-Pad!" Again, everyone still has a first-aid kit, but nobody uses them... no chance your child will get hurt when he/she is in the inert, catatonic state of down-loaded Nirvana.

Of course, we all know that maps are obsolete. Why? Because we now have SIRI or some other computerized pal telling us, "As soon as possible, make a U-turn." Why can't she just leave us alone when we stop to eat or to get gas?! Ah, well, such is progress. At least peace and quiet reign in the car — thank you, iPods and headphones.

"But the fruit of the
Spirit is love, joy, peace,
patience, kindness,
goodness, faithfulness,
gentleness and self-
control..."
Galatians 5:22-23

*Father, thank You for
giving us so many op-
portunities to demon-
strate the fruits of the
Spirit in our dear families.
Thank you for Your love,
patience, goodness and
faithfulness to us, your
undeserving children.*

ROME WASN'T BUILT IN A DAY

Some years ago, my husband won a sales contest and a trip to Rome, Italy. Wow! I was ecstatic. Deep within my pragmatic, provincial little soul, I had nurtured the fantasy to travel and to see the world.

Having grown up in a big, Italian family, I was especially excited. I am also a charter member of the "We May Never Pass This Way Again" club, so I wanted to ensure that we saw every church, art gallery, monument and fabulous ruin. Maybe Rome wasn't built in a day, but I wanted to SEE it in one day!

My husband later remarked, "If I don't make it home, I want my obituary to read: Death by Sightseeing!"

Anyway, I *was* right. We never made it back to Rome; but later we visited Italy again, this time to Sicily, where my grandparents were born. Our trek to our ancestral village of Bisaquino (20 miles west of Corleone, the birthplace of the Mafia, and easily accessible in our bullet-proof rental) was memorable.

The entire male population (about 23) was sitting around the town square playing cards and glaring at us like we were from the U.S. We knelt down, kissed their rings, swore Omerta, and promised never to try and speak Italian again.

In spite of our struggle with the language (due to acute "vowel impairment"), what a blessing to visit the home of my ancestors and to realize how far and deep those roots are. May our roots in Christ continue to grow as we look to Him as our Source.

"...and I pray that you, being rooted and established in love, may have power...to grasp how wide and long and high and deep is the love of Christ..."
Ephesians 3:17-18

Father, thank You for our parents, grandparents and all those who came before us who comprise our heritage. Most of all, thank You for the deep riches of our spiritual inheritance through Jesus Christ, our Lord.

what time is it there and what are you eating?

I well remember a discipleship group meeting when our pastor/leader asked us to list some life priorities/desires. We were young then and had not travelled much, so one of my husband's desires was to travel outside the country. Okay, LOL just doesn't do it here. Picture me rolling around the floor in hysterics. WHY? Because by the time my husband's career was complete, his passport resembled a small novel: Europe, Asia, South America, Africa, Australia. Sometimes, his jet lag had jet lag! "What time is it there, and what are you eating?" I'd always ask when he called, flicking off the crumbs of my latest peanut butter sandwich. I loved hearing about the wonderful cuisine, but also about the truly cringe-worthy sea urchin and 100-year-old eggs he was forced to eat (translate "swallow whole") so he would not offend his Asian customers.

He took me along a few times, but I could never compete with his Frequent Flyer miles! One of my priceless memories is the day my husband "requested" that I spend the day with the wife of his French sales manager while the two men conducted business. Since my French word for "butter" sounded exactly like my French word for "beer"... well, you can imagine that our conversation lagged a tiny bit. I smiled a lot that day. We are both so very humbled and grateful for all the travel opportunities we have had. To God be the glory!

"Delight yourself in the Lord and
he will give you the desires of your heart."
Psalm 37:4

"Now to him who is able to do immeasurably
more than all we ask or imagine....
to him be glory....forever and ever."
Ephesians 3:20-21

Father, thank You so very, very much for the opportunities you give us to see more of Your fascinating world and its people. We praise You that Your hand is clearly seen in the unfolding of world history.

Little ones to Him belong
This has been their nightly song
Full of mischief, fun and fire
Toe-to-toe and wire-to-wire
Never really far away
Prayers beseeching every day
Gram & Papa coming soon
Josh & Viv, you hung the moon

BEACH OR mounTainS?

When our children were growing up, we would usually go to the beach or to the mountains on our family vacations. One year, we did both, within a few weeks of each other. Why? I don't know. I didn't know then, and I still don't know. All I know is that my husband and I totally enjoyed our emotional break-downs. I'm kidding, of course.

As I was saying, sometimes we went to the beach, and we have such wonderful memories of eating sand, burning our eyes with salt water, roasting our skin, and clinging for dear life to our rafts until we reached full "beached whale" status on the shore — everything a beach vacation should be.

One time, we rented a house, and it rained every day. We decided my husband would just go back to work and rejoin us later in the week. What fun. The kids and I stared at the rain and at each other (and at the crayons and puzzles) with abject horror. Of course, I'm exaggerating. It really wasn't all that bad, unless you wanted to see the ocean, or see the sun, or see other PEOPLE. Then, there were the Smoky Mountains.

We loved going to Blowing Rock, North Carolina, where the scenery was majestic, the food great, the entertainment and activities delightful, and the weather always COLD.

ME: "No, I didn't pack any long pants or sweaters...this is JUNE!"
HUBBY: "We came in June LAST year and froze to death!"

Oh. For some weird reason, my husband thought Experience was a great teacher.

> **"Should you not tremble in my presence?**
> **I made the sand a boundary for the sea,**
> **an everlasting barrier it cannot cross."**
> **Jeremiah 5:22**

Father, we praise You for the sand and the ocean, for the majesty of the mountains and for Your visible glory in all Your creation.

DO CloTHES REally MAKE THE MAN?

My husband and I shared a laugh the other day when we heard someone on T.V. say that denim was making a comeback. Has denim ever been gone? In fact, isn't denim the new business suit of the modern workplace?

Of course, men's jeans have gone from Levis and Wranglers to Lucky and other urban looks; and women's jeans have gone from classic to sits-at-the-waist to low-rise, mid-rise and skin-tight, necessitating a brand name meant to comfort all women over the age of 40 — Not Your Daughter's Jeans. YAY!

But of course fashion has really changed over the years. Casual is the new Formal, accomplished by the addition of lace, beads, sequins, rhinestones and other embellishments to our T-shirts and jeans. Yep, what used to be reserved for night wear only has become our "go-to" breakfast ensemble. We have bid farewell to double-knit and welcomed Spandex into every category of our wardrobes. No kidding, why does every shirt I buy now fit me like a vise?

And no doubt, we are all thankful for "dry-fit" and "quick-dry" and "cool-FX" and "Sunscreen Factor 50" labels in our clothes. I mean, would the rain or sun DARE to bother us?

In spite of today's fashions, it seems people still seem to value comfort above everything. Witness the explosion of people wearing their pajamas in public! Really? Let's admit it. There's a nagging question in the back of all our minds — can we really be happy in anything but our sweatpants?

"The Lord does not look at the things man looks at.
Man looks at the outward appearance,
but the Lord looks at the heart."
1 Samuel 16:7

Father, forgive us for being so concerned with our outward appearance and how we look to others. Help us to desire the transformation of our hearts and minds above all else.

These Scales are way Off

How many times have you wished you could blame your old model dryer for the major shrinkage of all your clothes? Or stood in dread on that electronic demon otherwise known as a "health-o-meter" and thought, "This CAN'T be right!!"

Color me guilty. I think I have finally realized that eating ice cream every day tips the scales in favor of the ice cream.

So, yes, diet is key here, but we don't have to rely on Weight Watchers or Jenny Craig. What we SHOULD and MUST rely on is the old, "If it tastes good, don't eat it" diet. No, really, rice cakes and cottage cheese are delicious.

Additionally, the other component that should accompany our weight control efforts is exercise. Jogging, walking, swimming, hiking, tennis…just watch those calories melt off, right? I would love for someone to explain to me why jogging 10 miles only burns off the calories from five M&M's! How is that fair?

But I shouldn't complain. I need to appreciate and care for the raw material God gave me but also realize that spiritual food and exercise are way more important in my life. How much time do I spend reading my Bible or praying?

"For the kingdom of God is not a matter of eating
and drinking, but of righteousness, peace and joy
in the Holy Spirit."
Romans 14:17

"So whether you eat or drink or whatever you do,
do it all for the glory of God."
1 Corinthians 10:31

Father, help us to care for our bodies because they are "temples" of Your Holy Spirit. Even more, help us to desire the spiritual nourishment we need to walk in faith.

have you had your probiotic today?

Gosh, I love the health craze that is sweeping our country now. When we were raising our children, it was basically Flintstone vitamins twice a day. Now, our grandchildren wake up to the giddy anticipation of drinking aloe and downing industrial-strength probiotics. Nutritional supplements reign supreme as the kids realize that they will never, ever have to eat fruits and vegetables again.

Of course, I'm not serious. We all know that nothing can replace fresh fruit and veggies in our diets (all from Earth Fare or some other organic market, NATURALLY, and costing five times the supermarket price). But I truly do applaud the move to a healthier, more natural lifestyle….fresh air, sunshine, exercise, and absolutely NO ASPARTAME. That's right. Chuck the diet sodas, diet gum, and diet everything, unless they contain a natural sweetener. Farewell to corn syrup, soybean oil, Red Dye #2, nitrates, and, well, we all get it. Welcome, fellow label readers, to "farm-raised," "grass-grazed," and 200% natural.

Nevertheless, it is comforting to feel we are "returning to

the earth," so to speak. Hopefully, we are reversing the drastic health effects of the food processing revolution and going back to eating the way that God intended.

"Then God said, 'I will give you every seed-bearing plant on the face of the whole earth and every tree that has fruit with seed in it. They will be yours for food.' "
Genesis 1:29-30

Father, thank You for all the wonderful ways You provide for us. Help us to be good, wise stewards of the earth and all it contains.

hOnEY, YOU'VE GOT nO RhYThM

Like most families, we've had our share of medical issues through the years We've had lumps, bumps, tears, fractures, abrasions, contusions, most of these resulting from sports injuries or falls.

Then, there was the time our younger daughter broke her toe in a desperate, hysterical attempt to escape a flying roach! Sorry, Mandy.

We've also had a few surgeries and a couple of diseases—immune, auto-immune, and never-been-immune.

But the scariest medical emergency happened on the golf course one day when my husband announced on Hole No. 4 that he was dizzy and that his heart was beating 850 beats per second. Something told me this was more than just his awful putting. Off to the emergency room and to every test known to man that requires fasting for 92 hours. The results? Well, he was starving, of course! Seriously, the diagnosis was atrial flutter, which is a rhythm problem. But having danced with the man for all these years, I was not surprised! Just kidding, honey. The remedy was catheter ablation, a procedure that restored his heart rhythm and restored him to his lifetime post of Chief Commander & Supervisor... whew! What a relief.

But in all earnestness, I am so grateful to the Lord for His many answered prayers through the years on behalf of our family's health. We still contend with many issues, but He promises we can trust Him in all our circumstances.

May we spend our healthy days, as well as our struggling ones, in the Lord's service and for His glory.

"Therefore, we do not lose heart.
Though outwardly we are wasting away, yet inwardly
we are being renewed day by day."
2 Corinthians 4:16

Father, thank You that You are the Great Physician and for all the opportunities You give us to trust You in our lives.

ONCE UPON A WEDDING

For better or worse the vows that you make
And realize how LONG forever will take
The engagement is over; there won't be a trial run
You'll be married FOREVER — doesn't that sound like fun?
How quickly will pass that honeymoon sublime
Then it's wash, clean & cook, if hubby can find the time
So let's drink a toast to a wonderful new life
The bride takes a husband, the groom takes a wife
To a life together that will always inspire
'Cause that marriage license will never expire!

Wow, it seems like only 49 years ago that my husband and I vowed to love, honor and help each other vacuum and mop for the rest of our lives. I still have a vague memory of floating down the aisle and a few minutes later watching his knees give way (or was it his nerves?) And what about you? Have you ever imagined a wedding, planned a wedding, or, even more, PAID for a wedding? Yes, weddings are wonderful, beautiful, special. And because we have two daughters, we had the distinct thrill of facing near-bankruptcy twice. I do wish someone would explain to me why an event that takes a year to plan (and all your retirement savings) is over in 20 minutes. But it was worth it, and we have the $1,000 wedding albums to prove it.

"For this reason a man will leave his father and mother and be united to his wife, and they will become one flesh."
Genesis 2:24

Father, thank You for the sacrament of marriage and for the wonderful, inseparable union You intended it to be. Give us the grace to persevere through all the circumstances of our married lives and to reflect the love of Christ to the world.

hAPPY BIRThDaY...
REallY?

Happy birthday, dear friend, you've now reached an age
When your mind and body aren't on the same page
Your joints, bones & muscles are in major decline
And you've no idea where you misplaced your mind
You try to stay fit but your body pays no heed
As atrophy arrives with astonishing speed
Your hands aren't too steady, your vision's not good
Instead of high fashion, you're now wearing your food
You've slipped all your discs & your veins have collapsed
Can you really believe so much time has elapsed?
Yes, Gravity and Time will someday hit hard
And the only gusto you'll grab? Your Medicare card

You will notice this poem addresses advancing age. Whether you are 30 or 70, guess what? Your age is advancing. Thirty-year-olds, start flossing and using SPF150 NOW. Seventy-year-olds, be grateful for cataract surgery. But no matter how you slice the birthday cake, every birthday is special because it reminds us we have enjoyed another year of our Creator's tremendous blessings.

"All the days ordained for me were written in your book before one of them came to be."
Psalm 139:16

Father, thank You for creating us in Your image and for sustaining us through our journey on this earth. We praise You for every year You have given us and ask Your Spirit to enable us to live every day and year for Your glory.

ERIN GO BRAGH

Do you have any idea what "erin go bragh" means? Neither do I, and I'm NOT going to Google it, either. Sometimes it's just better to remain ignorant. Anyway, a few years ago, I was asked to write a poem for a Sunday School St. Patrick's Day dinner. Here it is, in all its Gaelic splendor.

St. Paddy's Day greetings to each lass and lad
Ye're here this fine eve and ye'll be ever so glad
T'will be the best St. Paddy's Day ye've ever known
And ye'll not even be kissin' the old Blarney Stone

Just a night to remember Irish legend and lore
How Paddy drove the snakes from that ancient seashore
How we leprechauns are magic, so ye better beware
Or ye'll all sure be leavin' with green skin & green hair

So let your Irish eyes keep smilin', rub a shamrock or two
It's time for some fellowship and Irish beef stew

Of St. Paddy and the Irish we've said plenty, it seems
So "erin go bragh" — whatever that means!

"Therefore, as we have opportunity,
let us do good to all people,
especially to those who belong to the family of believers."
Galatians 6:10

Father, thank You for the many opportunities You give us to enjoy the friendship and fellowship of other believers. Help us to encourage one another as we enjoy the special times of gathering together as Your people.

Valentine's Day

Nothing that funny about Valentine's Day. After all, it's a time for romance, flowers and Godiva, isn't it? Time for those little Necco conversation hearts with all the achingly clever sayings: "Kiss Me," "Be Mine," "True Love," or more currently, "Tweet Me." Anyway, I wrote a poem for a Sunday School Valentine's dinner (based on 1 Corinthians 13:4-7) and later used it at my daughter's wedding.

Love is patient, kind and true
By the grace which God imbues
Does not boast nor seek self-pride
But only in our Lord abides
Asks forgiveness when it fails
Grants the same when love impels
Celebrates the truth in life
Perseveres through trials & strife
A cherished hope, a tender shield
That never fails when spirits yield

A beacon in a darkened world
Example of His love unfurled
The bonds we forge, the vows we take
Ordained by God and not by fate
Nor 'ere will cease nor life unbind
Until God's love rules all mankind

"Dear friends, let us love one another,
for love comes from God. Everyone who loves
has been born of God and knows God."
1 John 4:7

Father, thank You for all the loves of our life — spouses, parents, children, grandchildren, relatives, friends. Thank you most of all for showing us Your love in the person of our dear Lord & Savior, Jesus Christ. Help us to emulate His sacrificial love.

THERE'S NO TIME LIKE ALL THE TIME

Admittedly, when I first contemplated the "R" word, I was a bit apprehensive. Then, Retirement actually arrived, and I was PETRIFIED!

Well, everybody, we all know why we're here
To celebrate retirement with laughter & cheer
No more hectic schedules with business overseas
Just travelin' through life with your dear spouse to please
No more market objectives, no more budgets to guide
You can cook, clean & wash with your mate by your side
You'll have leisure time now to golf or to fish
You can stay in your p.j.'s 'til noon if you wish
Your wife is o.k. with you home all the while
Just don't mess around with her time or lifestyle!

You know, I thought 24/7 with the Chief Commander General Supervisor might be a little much, but it really hasn't been all that bad. He lets me do my own thing, and I let him iron and cook breakfast. Works for me. Truly, though, it has been a real blessing to spend more time with my husband and best friend. (Oh, he vacuums and mops, too.)

> **"Every good and perfect gift is from above,
> coming down from the Father."
> James 1:17**

Father, thank You for the careers and successes You give us. We acknowledge that all our blessings are by Your hand and ask You to help us spend our time wisely.

ThE STOCKINGS aRE hunG

Two weeks before Christmas, it's a pretty safe bet
You're asking yourself, "Am I having fun yet?"
All those cookies to bake & the presents to wrap
Who even has time for a SHORT winter's nap?
You want to send cards, to hang stockings with care
But who'll fold the towels and the underwear?
You're trimming the tree and decking each wall
Shopping online and avoiding the mall
Children's programs, cantatas, parties all filled with glee
You're dashing and prancing — you need therapy!
All the planning & thinking; your brain is all numb
No hope for a vision of even ONE sugarplum
So away busy schedules & all these things that annoy
And hurry up, January, we can't stand all this joy!

I think we can all agree that the holidays can be stressful.
I decided years ago that I would at least eliminate Christmas
card elbow. Instead, I would compose one brilliant Christmas

letter chock-full of sparkling comments about our beautiful, talented children (and now grands), along with all their
remarkable accomplishments and exciting news about our
dreams, goals, careers, etc. Nah, not really. Hopefully, the
tongue stuck in my cheek all these years has brought a smile
to other cheeks. Speaking of which, we could not have a better reason to smile than understanding what this season rep-
resents — the birth of our dear Lord and Savior, Jesus Christ.
What a reason to slow down and celebrate!

**"For to us a child is born, to us a son is given... And he will be
called Wonderful Counselor, Mighty God... Prince of Peace."**
Isaiah 9:6

*Father, forgive us when we get caught up in the busyness of
this season. Help us to focus on the greatest
gift ever given — our Lord and our Redeemer,
Jesus Christ.*

how much DOES That TURKEY WEIGh?

Thanksgiving seems to be everybody's favorite holiday, and with good reason — no shopping, no presents to wrap, no decorating, no cards — just cooking.

Indeed, it is a time for wonder: I wonder if the turkey is done; I wonder if the turkey is overdone. Have you noticed that no matter how much your turkey weighs, it is NEVER done when you think it will be? Or, it's done TWO hours before you planned? Thank goodness for aluminum foil!

I always think of Thanksgiving as the holiday of the five F's: family, friends, food, fellowship, and football. One Thanksgiving, we rented a bus for my entire, football-crazed family to travel to one of the best college rivalry games in the country. One side of the bus dressed in crimson & white, the other side sported orange & blue. You've perhaps heard the term "choked." Yes, the crimson & white team lost a 24-0 lead, but a great time was had by all, especially those garbed in orange & blue (who deserved a lot of credit for their restrained snickering on the bus trip home).

But seriously, Thanksgiving engenders a spirit of immense gratitude. It is a time for humble reflection as we celebrate God's grace, love and goodness to us and to all our dear ones.

"Enter his gates with thanksgiving and his courts with praise; give thanks to him and praise his name."
Psalm 100:4

Father, we praise You for all You have done for us, but especially for our salvation. Thank You for Your grace and mercy through Jesus Christ our Lord.

Why Can't I Have a Dog?

I really feel as if I need to address the topic of "man's best friend," which never even became a passing acquaintance at our house. Yes, our kids always wanted a dog, and my dear husband did, too; but he always told them, "It's up to your mother." Well, they didn't get a dog, and I blame it on DNA. Specifically, I blame my mother.

In an incredibly weak moment, my non-doggy Mom arrived home one day with a dog for my sister, brother and me. We were thrilled. At long last — the adorable, overdue, uber fulfillment of all our canine longing: Pepsi. She lasted two weeks. My ultra-neat, plastic-still-on-the-lampshades Mom said she just couldn't take it anymore, (the hair, the poop, the barking) and thus ended Pet World at our house.

And what about our own children?

Well, we once had a pet gerbil named April. For my money, April looked like a rat; so I wasn't overly enthusiastic. But at least she didn't bark. Our younger daughter Mandy had a pet rabbit in college: Beavis. We liked Beavis, who hung around a long time chewing on lamp cords and depositing little pellets everywhere. But no dogs. Guess I'm not a pet person, but I have many friends and relatives who own and love their creatures. And I get that, because animals can be an endearing, enriching part of God's creation.

By the way, I've noted that the dogs my daughters bought for their own children all came with batteries.

"Are not five sparrows sold for two pennies?
Yet not one of them is forgotten by God."
Luke 12:6

Father, thank You for all creatures great and small that inhabit your marvelous creation, and for the comfort and enjoyment they bring.

Want to Be a Teacher?

When I was in my late thirties, I had a moment of complete and irreversible lunacy — I decided to go back to school and get my degree. And what did I major in? English. And just what was I going to do with an English degree? Teach, of course. Fill those restless, inquisitive, hungry teenage minds with poetry and Shakespeare. Yeah, okay.

They were restless and inquisitive, alright — what time is this class over? And the only thing they were hungry for was lunch. But I really did love the challenge; and I loved the students, especially the ones who didn't try to cause me bodily harm. While I tried to teach them the difference between nouns and verbs, my students tried to teach me the difference between teaching and insanity: nothing.

Anyway, my career was rewarding but brief, due to my family's ridiculous expectations of meals and clean clothes. Guess it's in the gene pool, though, because both of my daughters also majored in English... no dangling participles or split infinitives at our house! Truthfully, the years I taught were some of my most fulfilling and laid the groundwork for future endeavors, such as leading women's Bible studies.

I believed then and still believe that teaching is a crucial, worthy profession. What a privilege and responsibility to influence the minds and hearts of others.

> "We have different gifts, according to the grace given to each of us... if it is teaching, then teach."
> Romans 12:6-7

Father, thank You for all our teachers, especially those who have taught us Your word. Give us wisdom as we teach our children and grandchildren.

aS ThE CEntuRY TuRnS

For various reasons, the year 2000 really stands out to me. What a year — from the ridiculous to the ridonkulous.

First, there was the Y2K scare, in which our relationship with canned goods and bottled water became way too close and personal. Remember how you stayed up until midnight on December 31st, waiting anxiously for your computer to blow up? When it didn't, you smiled knowingly at your friends and smugly declared, "See, I TOLD you there was nothing to worry about."

Then came the Summer Olympics, in which NBC decided we were not worthy of live TV coverage of events but WERE worthy of videotaped coverage of Synchronized Diving (otherwise known as Really-Dumb-Looking Diving).

Then, of course, we had the 2000 presidential election (Bush vs. Gore), in which Rhode Island voters reportedly had trouble threading needles for their state's antiquated needlepoint tapestry ballot, called the process unfair, and demanded a rethreading. And after the nation was left "hanging" for what seemed like another century, the election was resolved; and we were all counting our blessings... and counting... and counting... and recounting.

> "Praise the Lord my soul; all my inmost being,
> praise His holy name. Praise the Lord, my soul,
> and forget not all His benefits."
> Psalm 103:1-2

Father, thank You for the 21st Century and for all Your continued blessings upon us, our families, our friends, and our country. Please raise up leaders who know, love and serve You.

MY CHROMOSOME OR YOURS?

We all admit that certain things are on the X Chromosome — shopping, baking, decorating — and of course the wildly popular whining and nagging. On the other hand, if we want something measured, glued, hammered, painted, or sawed, we look to the big, strong Y Chromosome.

For example, let's look at home renovations. From my experience, here's the way it goes. X: select wallpaper pattern or paint color. Y: remove trim, strip existing wallpaper, seal walls, apply primer, wait a few hours, apply at least three coats of paint, congratulate X on her color selection that appears to be somewhere between squash and pumpkin.

Continue on to floor renovation. X: select flooring. Y: remove furniture, prepare old floor, install new floor, inhale poisonous fumes, declare home renovations to be a shade more fun than surgery. If Y happens to be putting up new wallpaper, X will stand around with coffee or coke and supervise Y, constantly pointing out the bubbles in the paper, and revealing to Y at the very end that the pattern is 1/48th inch off in the cor-

ner. Isn't it just fantastic the way we complement each other?! Thank goodness for the Y Chromosome and the many, many Home Depot genes therein.

> **"So God created mankind in His own image,**
> **in the image of God He created them;**
> **male and female He created them."**
> **Genesis 1:27**

Father, thank You for creating us equally in Your image and for the different roles we have within Your kingdom. Help us by Your Spirit to fulfil our purposes for Your glory.

is that another moving van?

Did she fulfill her calling in life?
Otherwise known as The Portable Wife
The movers are here; she's scratching her head
Pack up the swimsuits or load up the sled?

New doctor, new dentist; she'll soon start the search
New school & new neighbors; gotta find a good church
And where is the hubby who caused this big mess?
He's traveling, of course; she's home in distress

From sunshine to snow and all else in between
She's asking the Lord what all these moves mean
Trust in Me, child, until your life's journey ends
You'll have priceless adventures & precious, dear friends

I have never penned truer words. Yes, we have moved
many times, but what a blessing to make new friends and

experience new places. If we could, we would do it all over again. Surely, Ruth's sincere pledge to Naomi should echo our own.

"But Ruth replied, 'Don't urge me to leave you or to turn back from you. Where you go, I will go, where you stay I will stay... where you die I will die, and there I will be buried.'"
Ruth 1:16-17

Father, thank You that You go before us in all our moves and prepare the way for untold blessings. We praise You for all our experiences and for every dear friend we have met along the way.

WITH FRIENDS LIKE THAT...

Do we treasure our friends the way we should? To do justice to this topic would require an entire book; I just want to mention a few friends and their sacrificial love on our behalf.

When we moved to Canada, we met Gerry & Gloria, who spent much time and energy teaching us to ice skate and ski. The results of their sacrifice: falls, scrapes, bruised ribs, torn ligaments, bloody lips. We loved every minute and are frequently reminded of these special pals as we struggle to get out of bed every morning.

Next, I must mention our longtime friends (college days), Peggy & John. We have enjoyed many trips together over the years, with an especially memorable 10-day trek in the Grand Tetons National Park and Yellowstone. Just goes to show you can travel together and still remain friends.

Anyway, one time when we had a choice between a room with a king-sized bed, fireplace, and incredible mountain view and a little bitty room with a huge closet overlooking the parking lot... yep, they gave up all that closet space just for us.

They're the best.

Seriously, we cherish all our precious friends and are so grateful for all their prayers, encouragement, support and fun through the years.

"Therefore, as God's chosen people... clothe yourselves with compassion, kindness, humility, gentleness and patience. Bear with each other and forgive one another."
Colossians 3:12-13

"A friend loves at all times."
Proverbs 17:17

Father, help us to appreciate and love the friends You have given us. Help us to become better friends by our prayers, encouragement, and example.

SUMMER'S OVER

The summer is over — kids thought it too brief
But the faces of parents are bathed in relief
No more sibling rivalry, no more fights to diffuse
No more desperate moms trying hard to amuse

No more popsicles dripping on the carpet or floor
No continual slamming of the front or back door
Oh the daily routine that each mom must revamp
That perpetual search for the perfect day camp

And those annual holidays at the cottage or shore
Where it's too cold to swim and the rains always pour
Where the boys run amuck and the girls simply whine
While Mom prays and Dad grits his teeth all the time

Or those treks to Vermont or to Walt Disney World
When the car seems to shrink as the insults are hurled
"Move over!" they scream — "You're sitting on my side!"

"Are we almost there, Dad?" Such an enjoyable ride

So much fun all these summer adventures afford
How can they incessantly claim they are "bored"?
Their favorite refrain — "I have nothing to do!"
Oh to glorious summer must we now bid adieu?

Must we consign to memory the summer that is past?
Is the fun really over — is school here at last?
As our children return to the halls they have trod
Let us gratefully acknowledge there really is a God!

Does this sound familiar? Unfortunately, not only is the summer that inspired this poem over, but their childhood is over; and it all happened in a few weeks…at least it sure seems like it. Treasure those "sticky" moments; they'll be over before you finish mopping.

"Sons are a heritage from the Lord,
children a reward from him…"
Psalms 127:3

Father, thank You for the gift of our children and for the many opportunities we have to teach them Your truths, no matter what age they are. Give us patience and perseverance, and give us Your wisdom and power to model godly behavior before them.

OIDER Than... WEII, YOU KNOW... DIRT

For you "younger" people, just read this, smile and smirk a little, then file it away for future reference (keeping in mind that the older you get, the less "future reference" you'll have). Here are the major indicators of old age:

1) *Body Failure.* Your muscles and joints will continually scream for ibuprofen. In addition, you will have high cholesterol, high blood pressure, high blood-sugar and LOW everything else.

2) *Memory Failure.* You can't remember names, faces, dates, where you left your car keys or where you left your mind.

3) *Mirror Failure.* You will pass by a mirror and stare in fascinated horror and pity at the stranger looking back at you.

But in the unlikely event you do not trust these signs of old age, you can rely on your young grandchildren to confirm the abominable truth.

Our seven-year-old grandson Josh: "Grammy, are you old?"

Me: "Well, do I look old?"

Josh: "Yes, you do!" (with rather too much enthusiasm, I might add).

Our precious little 4-year-old granddaughter Vivian: "Grammy, I just love your squishy arms!" Thanks, cutie. And, as Josh and Papa approach the deli at the local grocery store in their motorized cart, Josh warns the group of folks ahead: "Watch out! Old Man coming through!" Priceless.

As my hubby put it, "I knew I was going to get old, but I didn't know it would happen so fast."

"Since my youth, God, you have taught me, and to this day I declare your marvelous deeds. Even when I am old and gray, do not forsake me, O God, till I declare your power to the next generation, your might to all who are to come."
Psalm 71:17-18

Father, thank You so much for all the hours and days of our lives. Thank you for allowing us the privilege and joy of seeing our children and grandchildren grow through the years, and help us by your grace to remain steadfast in teaching them about You.

WE PaSSED THE FINal!

Hooray! Yes, we did it! We passed the final exam of parent-hood. You are no doubt wondering how we know this. Here-with the components of the Parenthood Final Exam:

1) Your children are still alive; i.e., you didn't strangle them, even though the opportunities were ample and frequent;

2) Your children like to spend time with you, which includes going out to dinner and vacations; and because of their eternal gratitude and affection for you, they still let you pick up the tab

3) Your children have bestowed upon you the reward for all your sleepless nights — MORE sleepless nights, in the guise of grandchildren.

I'm kidding. Grandchildren are the greatest EVER because none of the rules apply when they are at your home... nothing

wrong with ice cream and pound cake for breakfast. Oh, and our grand-kids love to go shopping with us because they understand our limits: none.

But of course, the very best feature of being a grandparent is this: you can return the grandkids when they are behaving badly, accompanied by the words of wisdom you have garnered from all those years of parenting, "Good luck."

"Only be careful, and watch yourselves closely so that you do not forget the things your eyes have seen or let them fade from your heart as long as you live. Teach them to your children and to their children after them."
Deuteronomy 4:9

Father, how we praise You for the gifts of our children and grandchildren. Thank You for Your grace and wisdom as we strive to guide them and to teach them to know, love and serve You all of their days.

In conclusion...

As I said at the beginning, this book was intended to make you smile. I hope you have been able to relate to some of my experiences, and I also hope and pray you have drawn closer to the Lord through the Scriptures and prayers included.

If you have never asked Jesus to be your Lord and Savior, you can receive His gift of eternal life now. Romans 10:9-10 states, "If you declare with your mouth, 'Jesus is Lord,' and believe in your heart that God raised him from the dead, you will be saved." Now, that's a reason to smile!

acknowledgements

I would like to thank my husband, John, for all his prayers, encouragement, and advice during this endeavor. I would also like to thank my family, who indirectly provided me with most of my material! I am especially grateful to my granddaughter, Lindsay, for her great illustrations. Finally, but most importantly, I want to thank my Lord Jesus Christ for His salvation and grace, and for all the smiles of my life.

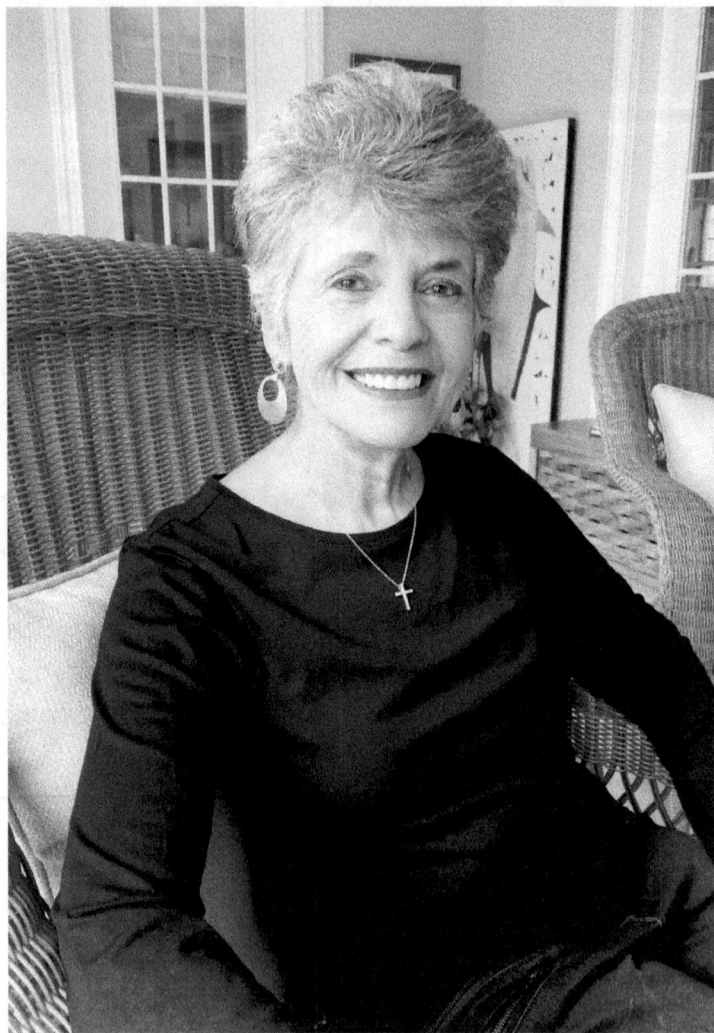

about the author
donna holland

Donna Holland is a graduate of the University of North Florida, a former English teacher, and a freelance writer.

Acknowledging that family is her greatest blessing, she collaborated on the illustrations for this book with her beloved granddaughter, Lindsay Blumenfeld. This is the first book for both. Donna says she's waited (and lived through) a lifetime of ups and downs to bring it to fruition - and hopes readers will enjoy reading it as much as she's enjoyed creating it.

The author resides with her husband, John, in St. Augustine, Florida and in Waynesville, North Carolina.

Additional copies of this book may be purchased through most online book retailers and by request through major and independent bookstores.

To purchase this book for your library, bookstore, school, store, or church, please contact the author at www.facebook.com/authordonnaholland.

www.ingramcontent.com/pod-product-compliance
Lightning Source LLC
LaVergne TN
LVHW021347080426
835508LV00020B/2148